Shojo Beat

# B.O.D.Y.

Vol. 8

Story & Art by

Ao Mimori

# Contents



## The Story Thus Far...

Ryoko falls hard for Ryunosuke, the quiet, bespectacled cutie who sits next to her in class. Then she learns that he moonlights as a host—a guy who dates women for money! Soft-spoken bookworm by day, aggressive ladies' man by night, Ryu may be more than the inexperienced Ryoko can handle. But she can't seem to get him out of her head...or her heart...

When pretty new teacher Miss Izumi shows a little too much interest in Ryunosuke, Ryoko learns that she used to be Ryunosuke's private tutor... and she taught him more than just English vocabulary. Worse, she's decided she has to have him back! As Izumi announces to Ryunosuke that she's in love with him, a boy who rides the bus with Ryoko confesses he has a crush on *her*. Will Ryu be tempted by Izumi... and would Ryoko be happier with a guy without quite so much baggage?

I'VE GOT A CRUSH ON YOU.
I'M FALLING FOR YOU.

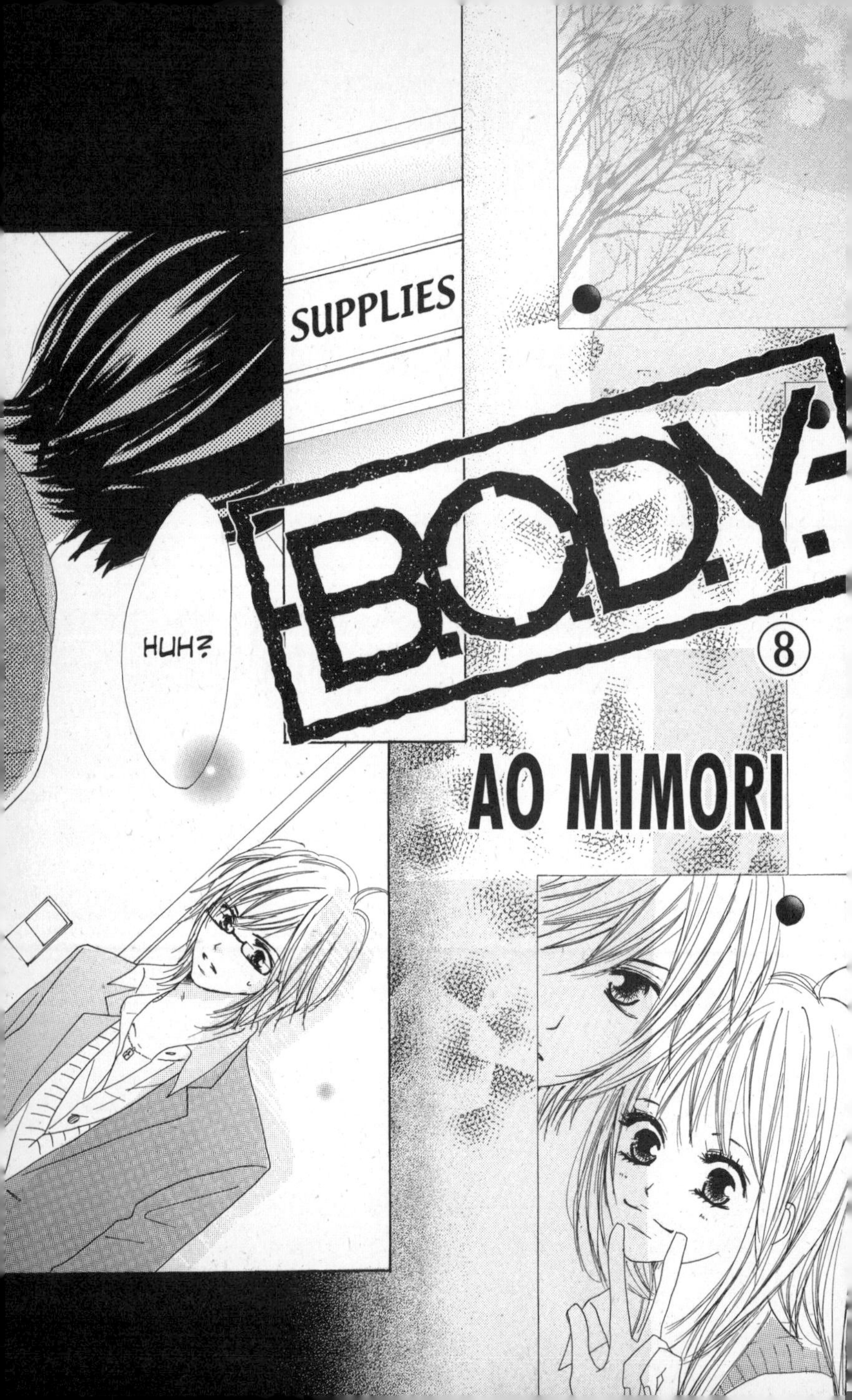
B.O.D.Y.
8
AO MIMORI
SUPPLIES
HUH?

WHAT'RE YOU TALKING ABOUT?
WHERE'D THIS COME FROM ALL OF A SUDDEN?
I KNOW, I KNOW.

I DIDN'T...
...EXPECT THIS TO HAPPEN.
I KNOW YOU HAVE A GIRL-FRIEND.
AND YOU DON'T EVEN *LIKE* ME.
BUT I CAN'T HELP IT.
I CAN'T STOP THINKING ABOUT YOU.

THIS IS IT, RIGHT? THE SUPPLY ROOM?
YEAH.
WHY DO WE HAVE TO...
...Get the print-outs...
CHAK
UM.
...
SHOVE
EEK!
S...
SORRY.
Let's go!
LET ME OUT.

① ✧

Hey, guys.
Ao Mimori here.
I'm about to slog through this author's note by talking about really unimportant stuff. If you've got time on your hands, please stick around.

SIIIGH

It's autumn already... Where did summer go? Did you guys go anywhere? I didn't leave the city. I stayed in Tokyo. Actually, I don't think I went anywhere besides the Suginami, Shinjuku and Chiyoda neighborhoods... and I stayed indoors most of the time. I really wanted to go to some summer music festivals. I wanted to have fun... SOB SOB

But it was a fun summer anyway. I know—if it was fun, why am I whining? Sorry.

Oh yeah!! Did any of you see it?

② WHAT? WHAT?

To be continued...

IS HE, LIKE...
I'VE GOT A CRUSH ON YOU.
...
BDMP
...ASKING ME OUT?
BDMP
WHAT NOW?
WHAT AM I SUPPOSED TO SAY?
UM...
...THANKS, I'M REALLY FLAT-TERED...

...BUT I'M ALREADY SEEING SOME-BODY.
I'M SORRY.
BOW
...
SO YOU...
...HAVE A BOY-FRIEND.
YEAH.
I SEE.

OKAY.
SORRY FOR SPRINGING THIS ON YOU.
AND THANKS FOR THE HANDKERCHIEF.
SURE...
ARE YOU KIDS GETTING ON THE BUS OR NOT?
Pssh

OH...
I'LL STICK AROUND HERE AWHILE. You go ahead.
THANKS FOR HEARING ME OUT.
VROOOM
BOW

THAT'S THE FIRST TIME A GUY EVER ASKED ME OUT.
WHAT WAS HIS NAME AGAIN?
KURAMA?
I WONDER HOW OLD HE IS.
I SHOULD'VE ASKED WHICH SCHOOL HE GOES TO.
NOT THAT...
BANG
BANG
...I'M TEMPTED OR ANYTHING!!
I SEE.
VROOOM

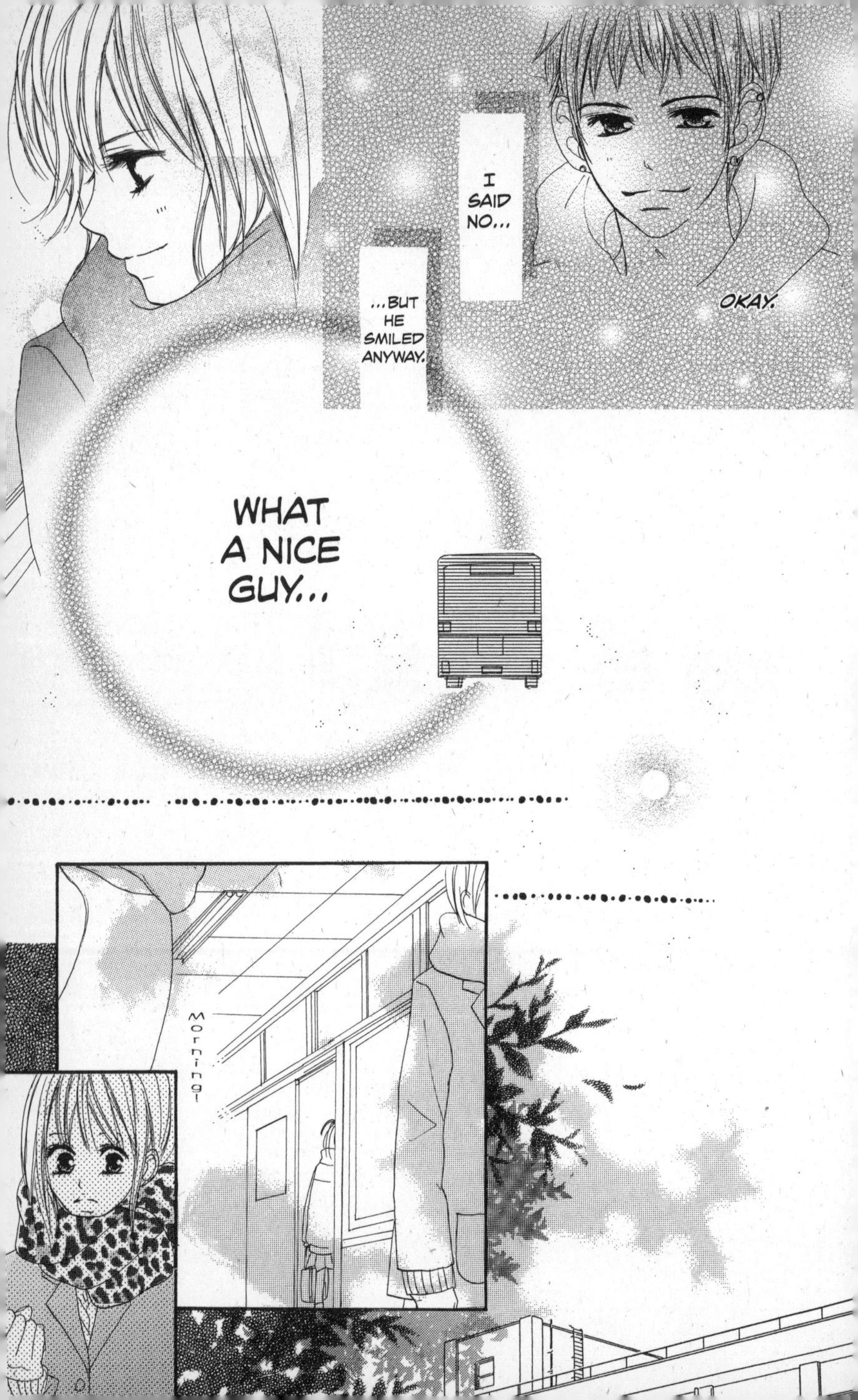
OKAY.
I SAID NO...
...BUT HE SMILED ANYWAY.
WHAT A NICE GUY...
Morning!

GASP!
MORNING, RYUNO-SUKE!
OH...
GOOD MORN-ING.
IS SOME-THING WRONG?
NO... I'M OKAY.
BUT *YOU'RE* REALLY BOUNCING AROUND.
WHAT?

WHAT WILL RYUNOSUKE SAY...
...IF I TELL HIM ABOUT YESTERDAY?
Some dude asked you out?
Where?
What's he like?
What'd he say?
Tee hee
I wonder if he'll get jealous...
...
HEY.
ACTUALLY, YESTERDAY...
FACULTY
PAF
PAF
FUJI!
HEY, SIR.
COME WITH ME.
HUH? WHY?
NO QUESTIONS.
SAKURA, GET TO CLASS.

What? I didn't do anything!
Just come with me.
WHAT'S UP WITH THAT?

2 — 2
RYOKO!
Detention first thing in the morning?
TAK
TAK
THERE YOU ARE!
HEY, GUYS!
WELL?
IS IT TRUE?
HUH? IS *WHAT* TRUE?
WHAT?

YOU HAVEN'T HEARD?
?
NO.
EVERY-BODY AT SCHOOL'S TALKING ABOUT IT.
THEY SAY RYUNO-SUKE...
...WAS ALONE WITH IZUMI-CHAN IN THE SUPPLY CLOSET.
WHAT?
SOME GIRLS SAW THEM.
THEY SAID IT LOOKED TOTALLY SUSPI-CIOUS. IZUMI WAS CRYING.
I DON'T KNOW HOW MUCH OF IT'S TRUE...

YOU HAVEN'T HEARD ANYTHING FROM RYUNOSUKE?
UM...
COME WITH ME.
NO, I HAVEN'T...
...BUT HE GOT SENT TO THE OFFICE JUST NOW.
WHAT?
FOR REAL?
WAH
WAH
THIS IS BAD NEWS...
SHH!
YESTER-DAY...
AFTER SCHOOL...
I GOT CALLED TO THE OFFICE AGAIN.
THAT'S WHAT HE SAID.
WHY?
DID HE MEET HER AFTER THAT?
OR WAS HE LYING ABOUT THE OFFICE?

DUDE, THIS IS SERIOUS.
HE COULD TOTALLY GET EX-PELLED.
Our school's got a zero-tolerance policy for that kind of stuff.
YEAH.
IT COULD HAPPEN.
Don't shoot your mouth off!
Ugh!
Zip it!
Eek!
shhk
EX-PELLED?
NO WAY!
THIS IS OUT OF CONTROL!
NOK
NOK
EXCUSE ME, SIR.
Go on in.
CHAK
PRINCIPAL

UH, HI.
WHAT'S THIS ABOUT?
ARE YOU FUJI?
I HAVE A FEW QUES-TIONS FOR YOU.

WE HEARD YOU WERE ALONE WITH MISS HIRANO YESTERDAY.
UH...
SOME STUDENTS SAW THE TWO OF YOU.
THEY SAID YOU WERE MEETING IN SECRET.
THERE ARE EVEN RUMORS THAT YOU'RE... *INVOLVED*.
HUH?
*YOU'VE GOTTA BE KIDDING ME!*
*THERE'S NO WAY!*
WATCH YOUR MOUTH, YOUNG MAN!
BOTH OF YOU...

...CALM DOWN.
I JUST WANT TO GET THE FACTS STRAIGHT.
MISS HIRANO ADMITS TO MEETING WITH YOU.
SHE SAYS YOU WERE JUST HELPING HER WITH SOME CHORES.
IS THAT TRUE?
...
UM, YEAH.
SIR! IF I MAY...
...THIS FUJI KID IS ALWAYS CUTTING CLASS!
YOU CAN'T TRUST WHAT HE SAYS!
SAME GOES FOR YOU, HIRANO!

I HEAR YOU LET SOME SLEAZY GUY HANG AROUND THE SCHOOL!
MAYBE YOU DON'T UNDERSTAND WHAT IT MEANS TO BE A TEACHER.
THAT DOESN'T MEAN YOU CAN COME TO MY WORKPLACE!
YOU JUST STARTED WORKING HERE, AND YOU'RE ALREADY CAUSING TROUBLE.
IF ALL YOU WANT TO DO IS *FOOL AROUND,* MAYBE THIS ISN'T THE JOB FOR YOU.
...
I'M SORRY...
...FOR THE INCONVENIENCE I'VE CAUSED THE SCHOOL.

I WILL ACCEPT ANY DISCI-PLINARY ...
THERE'S NOTHING BETWEEN ME AND MISS HIRANO.
WHAT'S WRONG WITH BEING ALONE WITH A TEACHER AT SCHOOL?

YOU'VE GOT SOME NERVE...
ALL RIGHT.
YOU MAY LEAVE.
BUT SIR...
WE HAVE NO EVIDENCE THAT ANYTHING INAPPRO-PRIATE HAPPENED.
BUT...
...IN THE FUTURE, TRY TO AVOID ANY ACTIONS THAT COULD CAUSE THIS KIND OF MISUNDER-STANDING.
IS THAT CLEAR?
YES.
YES, SIR.

WAH
WAH
COME TO THINK OF IT...
...RYUNOSUKE HAS BEEN KINDA WEIRD TODAY.
MAYBE SOMETHING DID HAPPEN...
CHAK
HEY...
TAKKA
RYUNOSUKE!

YOU'RE BACK FROM THE OFFICE!
WHAT WAS IT ABOUT?
HUH?
YOU'RE NOT GONNA GET *EXPELLED*, ARE YOU?
BUT EVERY-BODY'S SAYING...
OH, THAT?
I HAVEN'T DONE ANYTHING *THAT* BAD.
PAT
YEAH, RIGHT.
DING
DONG
I'LL EXPLAIN LATER.
...

BUT...
SIT DOWN!
Class is starting!
I'M GLAD...
SHK
...HE DIDN'T GET IN BIG TROUBLE.
BUT WHAT THE HECK'S GOING ON?

HYOO
WOO, IT'S COLD!
I shoulda brought my jacket.
IS THE RUMOR TRUE?
DID YOU SEE IZUMI-CHAN YESTER-DAY?
YEAH.
BUT I ONLY WENT TO SETTLE THINGS WITH HER.
HUH?

I WANTED HER TO STOP MESSING WITH US...
...SO I TOLD HER TO STAY AWAY FROM YOU.
IT WASN'T ANYTHING ANYBODY ELSE NEEDED TO HEAR.
SO I TALKED TO HER IN THE SUPPLY CLOSET.
RYUNOSUKE WAS ALONE WITH IZUMI-CHAN...
OH...
I SEE.
AWWW...
...MAN!
THUD
I GOT ALL WORKED UP OVER NOTHING!
YOU ALWAYS GET CARRIED AWAY.
PEOPLE WERE SAYING THE CRAZIEST STUFF!
I WAS FREAKING OUT TOO.
I didn't know what was up.

SORRY TO MAKE YOU WORRY.
... IT'S OKAY.
It wasn't your fault.
SO... PROBLEM SOLVED, RIGHT?
...
Um...
WELL...
...NOT TOTALLY.
WHAT?
WHEN I TALKED TO HER...
...SHE SAID SOMETHING TO ME.
I GUESS...

...SHE KINDA LOVES ME OR SOME-THING.
HUH?
DING
DONG
DOES THAT MEAN ...
...SHE ASKED YOU OUT?
KINDA.
YEAH.
OH, NO WAY!
SHE PROBABLY WASN'T SERIOUS.
I MEAN, HOW COULD SHE SAY THAT?
I don't believe it...
RYUNOSUKE!

WHAT IF SHE IS SERIOUS?
SHE'S NOT.
SHE'S ALREADY SEEING SOMEBODY.
SHE'S THE KIND OF PERSON WHO TOSSES WORDS LIKE THAT AROUND.
I'M JUST GONNA IGNORE HER.
...
THAT'S IT.
THAT'S MY FULL REPORT TO YOU.
Let's go back in.
It's freakin' cold today.
MISS HIRANO...

...LOVES RYUNO-SUKE.
LATER.
SEE YOU!
Bye!
JUST IGNORE HER.
I WOULDN'T WORRY IF IT WERE SOME RANDOM GIRL...
...BUT IZUMI-CHAN...
WHERE YOU GOING, RYOKO?
JUST OUT FOR A WALK.

...IS SOME-BODY SPECIAL TO RYUNO-SUKE.
CHK
HUH?
GASP
... Him!
WSSH
...

THUP
!!
HYOOOO
WHOA!
NOOO!
My guitar!
...
UM...
BRR BRR
...I'M NOT USUALLY THIS CLUMSY.
PFF ...
HE'S...
PFF ...
HEE...
NO, REALLY!

...KINDA FUNNY.
YOU HAD YOUR GUITAR YESTERDAY TOO, RIGHT?
ARE YOU IN A BAND?
UM, YEAH.
I'M ON MY WAY TO PRACTICE.
WHERE ARE YOU GOING?
ME?
NOWHERE IN PARTICULAR.
THINKING?
I WAS JUST...
...THINKING THINGS OVER.
YEAH.
SOME CRAZY STUFF'S GOING ON.
I WAS GOING OVER IT IN MY HEAD, GETTING MYSELF DOWN.

BUT YOU CHEERED ME UP.
COME TO THINK OF IT...
...I HAVEN'T LAUGHED LIKE THIS IN A WHILE.
I SEE.
WELL, GOOD.
I'M GLAD I DROPPED MY GUITAR.
Heh.
Thank God it didn't break.
HA HA!
WELL...
...HAVE A GOOD PRAC-TICE.
OH!

I USUALLY TAKE THAT BUS...
...SO I'M AT THE BUS STOP EVERY DAY AROUND THE TIME I WAS THERE YESTERDAY.
GIVE ME A SHOUT IF YOU WANNA LAUGH AGAIN.
IF YOU HEAR MY HORRIBLE GUITAR PLAYING...
...YOU'LL *DEFI-NITELY* LAUGH.
SURE.

You can't be that bad!
I'm godawful... My band-mates yelled at me the other day.
Ha ha ha...
Morning!
MORNING, IZUMI-CHAN!
BDMP

GOOD MORNING.
FIRST BELL'S ABOUT TO RING.
I KNOW.
GOOD MORNING, RYOKO.
GOOD MORNING.
I'M SORRY ABOUT WHAT HAPPENED YESTER-DAY.
IT MUST'VE WORRIED YOU.
I GUESS SHE KINDA LOVES ME...
NO.

I'M NOT WORRIED ABOUT SOME STUPID RUMOR.
I GUESS YOU'RE NOT.
AFTER ALL THE TROUBLE RYUNOSUKE WENT THROUGH YESTERDAY...
...YOU WERE OUT HAVING FUN WITH ANOTHER BOY.
WHAT?

TOK
I'VE...
...DECIDED NOT TO HOLD BACK ANYMORE.
I'M TAKING...
...RYUNOSUKE BACK.

I'M TAKING RYUNOSUKE BACK.
HUH?

TOK
WAIT A SECOND!
IS SHE SERI-OUS?
WHAT ...
...DO YOU MEAN BY THAT?

RYU HAD FEELINGS FOR ME FROM THE BEGINNING.
WHAT?
NOW...
...I KNOW I CHERISH RYU MORE THAN ANYONE ELSE.
YOU'RE NOT WORRIED ABOUT WHAT HAPPENED YESTERDAY...
...AND YOU SEEM TO BE STRINGING ANOTHER BOY ALONG.
IF THAT'S THE EXTENT OF YOUR FEELINGS...

...I THINK I CAN MAKE RYU HAPPIER.
WHAT THE HELL?
HUH?
HOW CAN YOU SAY SOME-THING LIKE THAT?

DING
THE THING WITH YOU TWO...
...WAS A LONG TIME AGO, OKAY?
DONG
RYUNOSUKE DOESN'T FEEL THAT WAY ANY-MORE.
AND THERE'S NOBODY BUT RYUNOSUKE FOR ME!
DING
YOU CAN'T WORM YOUR WAY IN, GOT IT?
GRR ...
SHE'S GOT ME SO PISSED!

I THINK I CAN MAKE RYU HAPPIER.
TAK TAK
HOW DARE SHE TALK TO ME LIKE THAT?
RYU HAD FEELINGS FOR ME...

DAK
GRAB
GOOD MORNING!
?
HEY...
...WHAT WAS THAT FOR?
What's wrong?
...
I'M NOT GONNA LOSE.
I DON'T CARE ABOUT THE PAST.
I'M HIS GIRL-FRIEND NOW.

What's wrong with hugging you?
Nothing. Do it anytime you want.
I'M NOT LETTING RYUNOSUKE GO.
HEY, RYUNOSUKE, CAN WE GO SHOPPING AFTER SCHOOL?
SURE, I DON'T MIND.
What're you gonna get?
CDs and...
...
HEY, ASUKA.
HUH?
Ooh, I got a text.
DON'T YOU THINK RYOKO'S ALL OVER RYUNOSUKE TODAY?

DING
WELL, DUH.
I MEAN, THEY *ARE* GOING OUT.
DONG
YEAH...
I guess, but...
CHAY
TODAY'S CLASS WILL BE IN THE AV ROOM.
LET'S ALL HEAD OVER.
GRP

WE'LL BE DOING LISTENING DRILLS TODAY.
AW, MAN!
NO WAY!
C'MON, GUYS, LET'S GET MOVING.
What do we need to take?
UM, RYOKO?
We gotta go.
GASP
OH!
Sorry, sorry...
I'M NOT GONNA LOSE TO HER.
THAT'S IT FOR TODAY.
AUDIOVISUAL ROOM

(2) Continued...
When I said "it," I meant the ad that went up in trains when volume 7 came out!! Any of you see it? I had a deadline and there was no way I had time to ride the train, so I didn't see it myself. I wish I had... It's not something that happens often.
It had a silver background and huge red lettering that said, "Can you love a boyfriend who used to be a host?" People keep forgetting that Ryunosuke was a host. Heh... I guess he's a normal high school kid these days. But I'm not sure what he'll be like in the future.
My writing's messy.

This is off the subject, but I've been getting mail from readers who hate Izumi. I kind of enjoy reading them. Ha ha ha...
I'm sure I'll get more after this volume...

(3) To be continued...

EVERY-BODY HAND IN YOUR WORK-SHEETS.
I don't want her near him.
I'LL TURN YOURS IN FOR YOU.
You've gotta go buy lunch, right?
OH.
Thanks.
TURN IN MINE TOO!!
Think I'll go...
...with a katsu sandwich.
I DIDN'T BRING LUNCH TODAY.
Help me out!
I GOTTA HURRY OR THEY'LL SELL OUT.
Ooh, me too!
WAH
WAH
ME TOO! THANKS!!
HUH?
HUH?
BADOOM
...
Melon bread!
Yakisoba sandwich!
TAK
TAK
...
FWIP

HMPH
YOU TWO...
...SEEM TO BE GETTING ALONG GREAT.
YOU REALLY SHOWED ME, HUH?
TAF
WHAT?
...
BY ANY CHANCE...

...IS RYU YOUR FIRST BOY-FRIEND?
!
...
WHY DO YOU ASK?
OH...
...YOU JUST SEEM SO *INEXPE-RIENCED.*
YOU WERE HOVERING OVER RYU LIKE A MAMA HEN.
TOK
YOU'RE SO... HOW SHALL I PUT IT? *PURE.*
SUCH AN INNOCENT RELATION-SHIP.
HOW CUTE.

SLAM
INNOCENT RELATION-SHIP...
CHAK
OH.
MISS HIRANO.
WHERE DID YOU PUT THE KEYS TO THE FILE CABINET?
AH!
I HAVE THEM!
I'LL BE RIGHT WITH YOU.
TAK

RYOKO?
AREN'T YOU GONNA EAT?
Lunch break's almost over.
YOU CAN HAVE MINE. I'M NOT HUNGRY.
SERIOUSLY?
I want the egg!
No fair!
HOW CUTE.

SUCH AN INNOCENT RELATION-SHIP.
...
WHAT'S WRONG WITH THAT?
YOU NEVER EVEN *HAD* A RELATION-SHIP WITH HIM.
DON'T LEAVE ME ALONE.
DON'T GO.
YOU ONLY HAD THAT ONE NIGHT.
WHO IS THIS GUY?
WELL...
BUT...
I DIDN'T WANNA BE REMINDED OF IT.
SHE WAS LONELY AND SHE *USED* ME.

IF HE GOT HURT, HE MUST'VE REALLY HAD FEELINGS FOR HER.
IT MIGHT'VE BEEN CASUAL FOR *HER*...
...BUT IT WAS SOMETHING SPECIAL FOR RYUNOSUKE.

I WISH I COULD...
...ERASE THAT MEMORY FOR HIM.
DING
DONG
PLIP
WHAD-DYA WANNA DO TODAY?
WANNA GET SOME-THING TO EAT?
BAM
OH.
YOU WANTED TO GO SHOPPING, RIGHT?

Let's go.
...
HUH?
I DON'T WANNA GO SHOPPING ANYMORE.
I WANNA GO TO YOUR PLACE.
FINE BY ME.
It's a mess, though.
I don't care.
IT'S OKAY.
I'M NOT DOING ANYTHING I DON'T WANT TO DO.
02
FUJI

Make yourself at home.
I'M GONNA GO CHANGE.
CHAK
OKAY.
CHAK
MESSY
...
It really is a mess...
WE'RE DATING.
IT'S ONLY NATURAL.

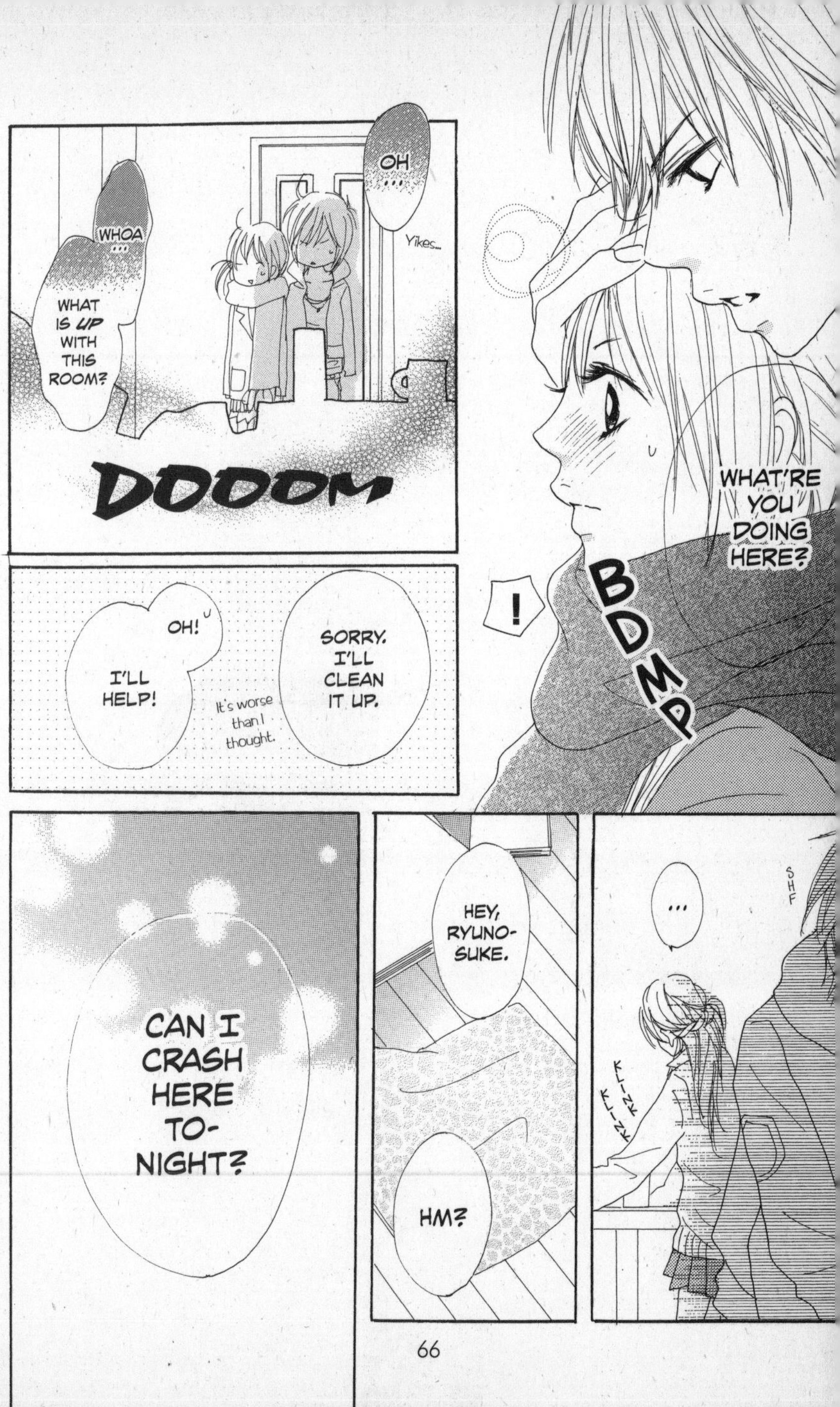
WHAT'RE YOU DOING HERE?
BDMP
!
OH...
Yikes...
WHOA...
WHAT IS UP WITH THIS ROOM?
DOOOM
SORRY. I'LL CLEAN IT UP.
It's worse than I thought.
OH!
I'LL HELP!
...
SHF
KLINK KLINK
HEY, RYUNOSUKE.
HM?
CAN I CRASH HERE TO-NIGHT?

WHAT?
DON'T WORRY ABOUT MY PARENTS.
I'LL CALL THEM LATER.
YOU DON'T WANT TO?
NO...
IT'S TOTALLY COOL WITH ME.
BUT WHY NOW?
...

HOW CUTE.
SHOOF SHOOF
WHY?
I DUNNO.
I JUST WANNA BE WITH YOU TONIGHT.

UM... DO YOU KNOW WHAT YOU'RE SAYING?
BDMP
DO YOU KNOW WHAT YOU'RE SAYING?
... YEAH.
SHF
I'M GONNA TAKE A SHOWER.

TAF TAF TAF
CHAK
I SAID IT.
BDMP
I TOTALLY SAID IT.
BDMP
BDMP
I THOUGHT I WAS READY...
...BUT I'M REALLY NERVOUS.
BDMP BDMP BDMP BDMP BDMP BDMP BDMP
BDMP

GUESS I SHOULD SHOWER...
FWP
!!
WHY DID I WEAR THESE PANTIES?
OOH LA LA!
Oh...
WELL, DUH.
I DIDN'T KNOW THIS WAS GONNA HAPPEN.
I just grabbed what was in the drawer.
I'D BETTER TAKE THAT SHOWER.
WAH
WAH
WAH
UM...
...WHAT DO I WEAR AFTER THAT?
I've only got my uniform.
ZERO EXPERIENCE
AM I MOVING TOO FAST?
Maybe it doesn't have to be today...
NO! NO HESITATION!
SPLISH
SPLISH

CHAK
I CAN'T BACK OUT NOW.
UM...
...I BOR-ROWED ONE OF YOUR TOWELS.
SURE.
No prob.

TAF
TAF
SHP
NOW...

...THERE'S NO OPENING FOR MISS HIRANO TO WORM HER WAY INTO.
I WON'T HAVE TO WORRY ANY-MORE, RIGHT?
...

...
SHF
RYUNOSUKE?
LET'S NOT.
LET'S NOT.
...
HUH?

WHY?
...
'CAUSE YOU DON'T REALLY WANT TO.
HUH?
... HOW DO YOU KNOW WHAT I...
YOU'RE TRYING TO *COMPETE* WITH HER, RIGHT?
!

OH NO...
WHAT?
WHAT NOW?
NOW...
...THERE'S NO OPENING FOR MISS HIRANO TO WORM HER WAY INTO.
I...
THAT'S NOT TRUE...
I REALLY DO...
...WANT TO...
WHAT WERE YOU THINKING WHILE WE WERE KISSING?
...DON'T WANT THIS TO BE CASUAL. NOT WITH YOU.

...
I'M SORR ...
GRP
TAK TAK TAK
CHAK
SLAM
I'M SO EMBAR-RASSED.
hff
hff

I'M SO EMBARRASSED I COULD DIE!
LET'S NOT.
I DON'T WANT THIS TO BE CASUAL. NOT WITH YOU.
I SHOULD'VE KNOWN THAT WAS THE WAY RYUNOSUKE FELT.
NO HESITA-TION!
BUT LOOK AT ME...
I CAN'T BACK OUT NOW.
PLIP

IDIOT!
I'M AN IDIOT.
RYOKO?
IT IS YOU!
TAKING THE BUS TODAY?

I AM TOO...
RYOKO?
ARE YOU OKAY?

HERE.
THANKS.
GET INTO A FIGHT WITH YOUR BOY-FRIEND?
WHAT?
YOU LOOKED SAD YESTERDAY TOO.
I KNOW IT'S NONE OF MY BUSINESS...
...BUT I'LL LISTEN IF YOU WANNA TALK ABOUT IT.
GRP
...

I...
...DID SOMETHING REALLY SELFISH.
HE REALLY CARED ABOUT ME.
BUT I DIDN'T REALIZE IT...
...AND I WENT KINDA CRAZY.
I'M AFRAID...
...HE'S PISSED AT ME.
BUT...
...YOU HAD YOUR REASONS, RIGHT?
"CRAZY"? WHAT'D SHE DO?
...
YEAH. A PATHETIC REASON.

ANOTHER GIRL...
...DECLARED WAR ON ME. SAID SHE WAS GONNA "TAKE HIM BACK."
WHAT?
SHE KINDA...
...HAS A PAST WITH HIM.
AND IT'S KINDA SPECIAL.
HE TOLD ME NOT TO WORRY...
...BUT I COULDN'T STOP.
I COULDN'T JUST SIT THERE AND DO NOTHING...

SHF SHF
Here. Tissue.
BLOW YOUR NOSE.
...
EROS EROS
TELEPHONE SERVICE
LONELY HOUSEWIVES
A HOT HOUSEWIFE IS WAITING AT THE OTHER END OF THE LINE
SEE BACK FOR DETAILS
NO!!
THIS ISN'T WHAT IT LOOKS LIKE!!
I'm not into milfs!
CRM
CRM
CRM
THEY WERE JUST HANDING THEM OUT...
VYOOO
SHING
...
Don't litter!
PET...
...
I THINK...
...YOU'RE JUST GONNA HAVE TO TRUST HIM FOR NOW.

WHAT?
IT'S NOT LIKE YOU CAN STOP YOURSELF FROM WORRYING.
BUT HE HASN'T GIVEN YOU ANY REASON TO, RIGHT?
YOU SHOULD STAND TALL. BE, LIKE, "I'M HIS GIRL-FRIEND NOW, BITCH!"
STAND TALL...
I'M HIS GIRL-FRIEND...
YOU'RE RIGHT.
I'LL DO MY BEST TO FEEL THAT WAY.
YEAH.
AND ON THE OFF CHANCE IT DOESN'T WORK OUT...

...THINK OF ME.
I'LL BE WAITING.
I'LL BE...
...HERE FOR YOU.

I'LL BE...
...HERE FOR YOU.

WAS THAT...
WHAT?
FORGET IT.
I JUST GET THE FEELING YOU'RE GOING THROUGH A ROUGH TIME.
IF YOU EVER WANNA GET AWAY FROM IT...
...I WANT YOU TO KNOW I'M THERE FOR YOU.
TO BE HONEST...
...I'LL PROBABLY STILL HAVE A THING FOR YOU.

KURAMA...
SHF SHF
HERE.
TO RYOKO
I'VE BEEN MEANING TO GIVE THAT TO YOU.
I'M PLAYING A SHOW PRETTY SOON.
IT'S A TICKET.

I WROTE THE DATE AND ADDRESS INSIDE.
A SHOW?
WE REALLY SUCK... BUT...
...COME CHECK US OUT IF YOU...
HEY, LOOK!
KURA'S WITH A GIRL!!
THIS IS RARE!!
BWA HA HA
YO!
SHE'S WEARING THE S HIGH SCHOOL UNIFORM...
BDMP
?!
S HIGH SCHOOL, HUH?
IS SHE...
WAAAAAA!
AIEEEE!
UM, ER...
...I GOTTA GO.
SHIELD
OKAY...

YOU CAN...
...TOSS THAT IF YOU WANT.
UM...
TAKKA TAKKA
So long!
You guys are dead!
...
Dear Ryoko,
Come by if you have time. You might have some fun. I'll be waiting.
Kurama
To Ryoko

③ Izumi!
Continued...

The letters basically read, "Izumi, die!"♡ You get the idea... ha ha!

But I personally don't hate her. That said, it's Izumi who gives me the most trouble when I'm writing rough drafts. I get frustrated all the time. I think, "Why won't she do as I say?"

GAAAH!

And the other new character, Kurama... Unpopular!! Nobody likes him!! Ha ha ha! "Anybody who gets between Ryoko and Ryunosuke needs to disappear!" That's basically the reason people give for hating him. He's different from what I originally imagined, but I'm happy with him.

Drawing Kurama's friends is fun. I like boys hanging out together. Drawing the band is hard work, though.

④ To be continued...

STUDIO ROT
LIVE
STUDIO ROT
LIVE BANDS
ECONOMY
SUPER CAP
SAILOR
1,500 YEN
DRINK
DOORS: 5:30 –
WHAT SHOULD I DO?
With this?
I'LL PROBABLY STILL HAVE A THING FOR YOU.
...
HOLY CRUD...
...I JUST TALKED ABOUT MY BOY-FRIEND TO A GUY WHO ASKED ME OUT.

Second time
WUP WUP WUP
NO! NO!
I'M NOT TEMPTED!!
IT'S JUST...
...
'CAUSE YOU DON'T REALLY WANT TO.
I WAS IN SHOCK.
HUH?
...
HOW DO YOU KNOW WHAT I...
YOU'RE TRYING TO COMPETE WITH HER, RIGHT?
!
WHAT WAS I THINKING?
...DON'T WANT THIS TO BE CASUAL. NOT WITH YOU.
SHIIIN
...
I WONDER IF RYUNOSUKE'S MAD.
I SHOULD PROBABLY CALL HIM.
HE HASN'T TEXTED ME.
THIS IS ALL MY FAULT, REALLY.
PIP
PIP

CAN I CRASH HERE TONIGHT?
BLUSH
WOO
ARRGH!
CHIRP
CHIRP
AFTER LAST NIGHT...
...I DON'T KNOW HOW TO TALK TO HIM!

NO SLEEP
RYUNOSUKE NEVER CALLED.
HOW CAN I FACE HIM?
HEY.
DON'T BRUSH ME OFF.

RYUNOSUKE ...
...
GRP
COME HERE. C'mon.
HUH?
WHERE ARE WE GOING?

I GOTTA TALK TO YOU.
BDMP
I GOTTA TALK TO YOU.
ABOUT WHAT?
WHY DOES HE HAVE TO PULL ME ASIDE?
BDMP
HE'S NOT BREAKING UP WITH ME, IS HE?
BDMP
OH, NO WAY!
What's going on?

TUP
WHAT NOW?
LISTEN...
BDMP
ABOUT YESTER-DAY...
LOOK, I'M TOTALLY SORRY!

WHAT?
I THOUGHT ABOUT CALLING YOU SO MANY TIMES...
I DIDN'T KNOW WHAT TO SAY.
...BUT I THOUGHT YOU'D BE DISGUSTED WITH ME.
I'M SORRY I DID SOME-THING SO DUMB!

DON'T STEAL MY LINE.
I WAS GONNA APOLOGIZE TO *YOU*.
I'M SORRY ABOUT YESTER-DAY.
I SAID SOME CRAPPY THINGS.

WHAT?
WHAT ARE YOU SORRY FOR?
...
I WASN'T THINKING ABOUT HOW YOU FELT.
YOU WERE REALLY WORRIED, RIGHT?
I DIDN'T HAVE TO GO AND SAY YOU DIDN'T REALLY WANT TO...
...OR THAT IT WAS CASUAL.
I'M SORRY...
DON'T BE!

EVERY-THING YOU SAID WAS TRUE.
AND...
I DON'T WANT THIS TO BE CASUAL.
...I'M GLAD TO KNOW...
...YOU'RE SERIOUS ABOUT ME.
SHEESH.
I'M THE ONE WHO'S SORRY.
NO... I AM TOO.
SORRY.
...
GRP

CHU
SO WE'RE BOTH SORRY.
THAT MAKES US EVEN.
...
OKAY.
WHAT A RELIEF.
...

HEY.
HM?
WE'VE BEEN GETTING INTO A LOT OF FIGHTS LATELY, HUH?
WHAT?
EVER SINCE *SHE* SHOWED UP.
BDMP
...
YEAH.
ANYTHING I CAN DO TO HELP?
HUH?

POP
WE CAN HANG OUT ALL THE TIME AT SCHOOL...
...OR ALWAYS HOLD HANDS.
What?
NO! THAT'D BE EMBARRASSING!
WHAT'S GOTTEN INTO YOU?
I DON'T CARE IF IT'S EMBARRASSING.
IF IT'LL MAKE YOU FEEL MORE SECURE...
...I'LL DO ANYTHING.
Just say the word.
RYUNOSUKE...
YOU DON'T HAVE TO DO ANYTHING.

THOSE WORDS...
...ARE ENOUGH.
YUP. ♡
PFF
...
MAYBE YOU'LL FEEL EVEN MORE SECURE...
I won't stop you this time.
WANNA PICK UP WHERE WE LEFT OFF YESTER-DAY?
BDMP
!
YOU'RE THINKING ABOUT THAT THIS EARLY IN THE...
EEK!

WHAT TIME IS IT?
IT'S 9:15.
SCHOOL!
Oh no!
FACULTY ROOM
After school
YOU WERE AN HOUR LATE...
SIIIGH
...AND FUJI NEVER SHOWED UP.
TP
TP
YOU SAID HE'D COME IN AT NOON.
You know it's al-ready four, don't you?
THAT'S WHAT HE TOLD ME!
That's weird...
YOU CAN'T GO HOME!!
I was up all night.
I'M SLEEPY.
I only got up to talk to you.
EVERY-BODY'S SLEEPY IN THE MORNING!
AW, FINE. I'LL GO IN AT NOON.
SHUP
SLAM
HE GAVE ME ALL THE BUSYWORK HE COULD FIND.
SHF
SHF
HAVE IT ALL DONE BY TOMOR-ROW.

Hey!
To Ryoko
Come check us out...
OH YEAH!
WHAT SHOULD I DO WITH THIS?
I'VE HAD A CRUSH ON YOU.
I'LL BE WAITING.
IF I GO...
...IT'LL GIVE HIM THE WRONG IDEA.
I SHOULD JUST GIVE IT BACK.
SENT TO THE OFFICE, HUH?

UGH ...
HMPH
...
HM?
SORRY, AM I WRONG?
SHUK
DON'T CAUSE TOO MUCH TROUBLE FOR HIM.
CAAW CAAW
...
CRACK
MR. SASAKI'S ALWAYS SAYING...
..."SAKURA SEEMS LIKE A NICE GIRL, BUT SHE'S A HAND-FUL."
Guess he's right.
Mr. Sasaki

THAT WOMAN REALLY GETS ON MY NERVES !!
Why, couldn't she just walk on by?
UGH UGH UGH
HA HA HA
M CITY HIGH SCHOOL
I'M GONNA GIVE THIS TICKET BACK AND GO STRAIGHT HOME.
AND MR. SASAKI TOO.
HE'S GOT A BIG MOUTH.
Even if it's true...
I THOUGHT HIS FRIENDS WENT HERE.
They wore this uniform, right?


Both street clothes and uniforms are allowed.

S High, maybe?
Whose uniform is that?
SHK
SHK
COME TO THINK OF IT...
...MAYBE THIS WAS A BAD IDEA.
...
I CAME HERE 'CAUSE I DON'T HAVE HIS NUMBER...
...BUT MAYBE HE'S ALREADY LEFT.
I'M GOING HOME.
HEY...

SHING
OH!
WHAT'RE YOU DOING HERE?
WEREN'T YOU WITH KURA THE OTHER DAY?
HEY! His friend!
YEAH...
DID YOU COME HERE TO SEE KURA?
HUH?
COME HERE TO SEE KURA...
HE MAKES IT SOUND LIKE I'VE GOT A THING FOR HIM.
I SHOULDN'T HAVE COME.

NO.
I WAS JUST PASSING BY.
SHU!!
QUIT WALKING SO FAST!
I'm carrying a bunch of crap!
HEY...
I know her.
HEY!
YOU'RE THAT GIRL!
YEAH!!
THAT'S RIGHT!!
YOU'RE KURA'S RYON-RYON!!

RYON-RYON?
What the heck?
KURA!!
RYON-RYON'S HERE!!
Get your ass over here!
UM...
...RYON-RYON?
No way.
UH...
YEAH.
IT'S RYON-RYON! SERIOUS!!
WE HEARD YOUR NAME WAS RYOKO, SO...
THEY GAVE ME A NICK-NAME!!
It is me!!
HURRY UP, KURA!
YEAH, RIGHT. LIKE SHE'D COME AROUND HERE.
You're always ragging on...

?!
No way!
HEH HEH
...
HEH HEH

SORRY WE DRAGGED YOU HERE, RYON-RYON...
WAK
QUIT CALLING HER THAT!!
...
I'M SO SORRY...
...MY JERKY FRIENDS CALL YOU THAT.
OW, MAN!
I'LL MAKE 'EM STOP.
NAH.
It's no biggie.
DON'T WORRY ABOUT IT.
REALLY?
YOU'RE SO NICE, RYON-RYON! ♡
I think I'm falling in love!
ARRGH
SHUT UP, MAN!!
ARRGH
Me too!
SORRY WE'RE SO IMMATURE.
We're total freaks.
ER...
Hey!
DID YOU HEAR WE'RE PLAYING A SHOW TOMORROW?
BDMP
!
...
YEAH.
NO... DON'T BRING THAT UP NOW...
YOU GAVE HER A TICKET, RIGHT, KURA?
YEAH.

Oh!
THAT'S WHY YOU'VE BEEN ACTING WEIRD!!
YOU'RE SO EASY TO READ.
WHAT?
HE USUALLY SLACKS OFF AT REHEARS-ALS.
SO I WONDERED WHY HE WAS PRACTICING DURING LUNCH TODAY.
FOR ME?
IT WAS FOR YOU.
Now I get it.
SHUT UP!!
TWITCH
SORRY, RYOKO.
WE SHOULDN'T HAVE COME HERE.

I'D WALK YOU HOME...
...BUT WE'VE GOTTA GET TO PRACTICE.
OH, THAT'S OKAY.
I'll be fine.
WHAT? Leaving already?
SHUT UP!
BOO
I wanna hang out with Ryon-Ryon!
BOO
Throw mine away too.
I WONDERED WHY HE WAS PRACTICING DURING LUNCH.
IT WAS FOR YOU.
KSH
...
WHAT SHOULD I DO WITH THIS TICKET?
SORRY AGAIN.
ERK
PRETTY ANNOYING, HUH?
SHF
OH...
NO.
Really?
GOOD.

HEY, COME TO THE SHOW.
BDMP
WE ALL KNOW YOU ALREADY REJECTED KURA.
You've got a boyfriend, right?
HE DOESN'T HAVE ANY EXPECTATIONS.
BUT...
...YOU OUGHTA SEE THE HARD WORK HE'S PUT IN.
You remember all the chords?
Heck yeah!
LATER, RYON-RYON! WE'LL SEE YOU AT THE SHOW!
...
...

I COULDN'T GIVE IT BACK AFTER ALL.
ARGH
NOT AFTER HEARING THAT.
YOU OUGHTA SEE THE HARD WORK HE'S PUT IN.
WHAT SHOULD I DO?
HUH?
ARE YOU SERI-OUS?
You bet.

RYOKO ...
WHAT'S GOING ON?
PERFECT TIMING.
YOU SHOULD HEAR THIS TOO.
THE WAY THINGS ARE GOING, FUJI'S IN REAL DANGER OF REPEATING THE YEAR.
HUH?
Man...
SO, STARTING TODAY, HE'LL BE TAKING REMEDIAL CLASSES IN THE SUB-JECTS HE'S CLOSE TO FAILING.
Here's your schedule.
How'd this happen?
Repeating the year?
He could get held back.
There's always one person every year.
SKIP OUT THIS TIME AND YOU'RE *NOT* MOVING ON.
AND I DON'T WANT YOU ABSENT FOR *ANY* REASON BESIDES ILLNESS.
I'm warning you.
HELP HIM WAKE UP AND SMELL THE COFFEE, SAKURA.
DING
DONG

I DIDN'T KNOW IT WAS THIS BAD.
Yikes.
RYUNOSUKE...
...CAN YOU DO THIS?
It's every day.
AW...
I'LL SUCK IT UP.
I WANNA BE A SENIOR WITH YOU.
OKAY.
I'LL HELP YOU GET UP EVERY DAY.
WHAT TIME?
NAH, FORGET IT. YOU'RE ALWAYS CUTTIN' IT CLOSE TOO.
Not anymore.
SHOOF

TO RYOKO
BRRRRING
SLAP
RYUNO-SUKE!
WAKE UP! IT'S SEVEN!
CHIRP
CHIRP
...YEAH ...
...YEAH ...I'M UP...
YOU'RE NOT GOING BACK TO BED?
REALLY?
...
RYUNO-SUKE?
... ...
ZZZ...
RYUNO-SUKE!!
I can hear you snoring!!

WILL HE SHOW UP?
Morning!
Morning!
SAKURA.
HI.
DID YOU WAKE HIM UP?
Wow, it's cold.
I TRIED.
He might've fallen back to sleep.
MAYBE I SHOULD HAVE GONE TO HIS HOUSE...
...

Oh well.
AT LEAST HE'S GOTTEN BETTER SINCE HIS FIRST YEAR.
HUH?
HE DIDN'T HAVE ANY CLOSE FRIENDS BACK THEN.
I was his homeroom teacher.
AND HE DIDN'T TAKE SCHOOL SERIOUSLY, SO IT WAS HARD GET-TING HIM TO SHOW UP.
BUT NOW HE'S MAKING AN EFFORT FOR YOU.
I WANNA BE A SENIOR WITH YOU.
OH.
YEAH.
IS THIS YOURS?
SHF
SHF
HEY!
HOW'D YOU GET THAT?
SOME-BODY FOUND IT.
You're the only Ryoko in class...

WHEN DID I DROP IT?
THE TICKET'S STILL IN HERE.
THANKS.
HEY...
CHK
WAS THERE A NOTE IN HERE?
DON'T KNOW.
I didn't look inside.
...
MAYBE IT JUST FELL INTO MY BAG.
Oh well.
HEY!
THERE HE IS!
REALLY?
RYUNO-SUKE!
WAAH

GOOD MORNING.
All right!!
Nothin' good about it...
Yes!
CHING
Dear Ryoko,
Come by if you have tin
You might have some f
I'll be waiting.
Kurama

THERE'S NOBODY ELSE BUT RYUNOSUKE FOR ME!
...
Can't... open eyes...
Come on!
LIAR.

# Once again... hello!

How're you all doing? Ao Mimori here! ♡
This is the eighth volume of B.O.D.Y.! Thanks for helping me make it this far!!
It's a little intimidating... but thanks anyway!♡

I had a lot of great experiences this summer, like working on the release of the B.O.D.Y. drama CD and appearing on a radio show.♡ The radio show was recorded at Kudan Kaikan. There were about a thousand people in the audience and a lot of famous voice actors appeared on the show. My heart was pounding... Yeah, I was a little nervous. Can you blame me? It was fun to be part of the action.

The recording for the drama CD was also a lot of fun...♡ It was like a dream. The CD includes a roundtable I did with Junichi Suwabe, who played Ryunosuke, and Tomoko Kawakami, who played Ryoko, so please give it a listen!! There's more about my summer adventures in the bonus manga at the end of this volume.

Page 132 and 175 — Radio Recording Diary
Page 176 — Drama CD Recording Diary & Comments

They're not too long. I hope you read them.

Okay, let's do this...

LIAR.
Dear Ryoko,
Come by if you have time. You might have some fun. I'll be waiting.
Kurama
Hey, wake up!
The bell's gonna ring!

# Radio Recording Diary Part 1!!

THE TWO HOSTS OF SHÛEI GAKUEN OTOME KENKYÛBU!!
TATSUHISA SUZUKI
JUNICHI SUWABE
Vaguely remembered costumes
DOOM
Scientist (w/ explosive boob padding)
Maid
SUPER FAMOUS VOICE ACTORS!!
MASAYA ONOSAKA
KÔSUKE SHIMAUMI
YOSHIHISA KAWAHARA
TAITEN KUSUKINO
MIKAKO TAKAHASHI
TOMOKO KAWAKAMI
BAAM
Whoa, these look nothing like them... I apologize to the fans...
AN AUDIENCE OF 1,000!!
3F
2F
1F
ZOOOM
SUPER NEWBIE!!
Ao Mimori
...
YEEK!
I... I'M...
...AO MIMORI, CREATOR OF B.O.D.Y. ...
TOMOKO KAWAKAMI
VOICE ACTORS
MIC
SPEAK INTO THE MIC!!
STIFF
Bring it closer to your mouth!
I DON'T REMEMBER WHAT I TALKED ABOUT.
ACTUALLY, MY MOUTH BARELY MOVED.
MORE ...

DING
DONG
So long!
Let's hit the arcade!
Ha Ha Ha
I'm hungry!
...
RYUNO-SUKE!

ISN'T IT ALMOST TIME FOR REMEDIAL CLASS?
KAAW
KAAW
...
HMPH
I SO WANNA GO HOME.
WHAT?
YOU CAN'T SKIP OUT!
IT'S ONLY THE SECOND DAY!
Stop sulking!
C'MON, MOVE IT!
WHAT'S TODAY'S CLASS?
WUP
If you get held back, you'll be in the same class as Kousuke!
WUP
Sigh...
I DUNNO... I HAVEN'T LOOKED AT THE SCHEDULE...
Shirai... ugh...
YOU'RE GONNA FLUNK!!
BUT WHEN I THINK...
...ABOUT HAVING TO LIVE LIKE THIS FOR WEEKS...
I'm tired... I can't hang out...
BUT YOU'VE GOTTA DO IT! WE'LL GET THROUGH THIS!

WE'RE GONNA BE SENIORS TOGETHER, RIGHT?
Um...
YOU'RE GOING TO CLASS, SO I'LL JUST GO HOME AND DO SOME HOMEWORK.
I need to catch up too.
...
Then get ready.
YEAH.
WHAT'RE YOU GONNA DO TODAY?
WHAT?
I'M SORRY.
WE CAN'T HANG OUT, YOU GOTTA WAKE UP EARLY...
HUH?
NAH, IT'S ALL RIGHT.

I'M YOUR GIRL-FRIEND.
It's my job.
BESIDES, ONCE THIS IS OVER, WE CAN HANG OUT ALL WE WANT.
'BYE!
OKAY.
Study hard!
Be careful!
SKIP OUT THIS TIME AND YOU'RE NOT MOVING ON.
HE'S REALLY DOING IT.
HE EVEN CAME IN ON TIME TODAY.
WHEW
I HOPE HE CAN GET THROUGH THIS...

GUIDANCE COUNSELOR
CHAK
TAK
TEN MINUTES LATE.
YOU'RE EVEN LATE TO REMEDIAL CLASS.
Sheesh.

ANY OTHER TEACHER WOULD BE FURIOUS.
UH-OH. ENGLISH.
TOK TOK
I'M SORRY.
WE CAN'T HANG OUT...
I TOLD HIM IT WAS ALL RIGHT...
...
...BUT IT IS KINDA LONELY.
GUESS I'LL TAKE THE BUS TODAY...
GASP ...

I'M PLAYING A SHOW...
HANG ON.
I THINK THAT WAS TODAY...
SHK SHK
It is today!
...
WE REALLY SUCK.
You remember all the chords?
Heck yeah!
COME CHECK US OUT.
TOSS THAT IF YOU WANT.
I'M NOT GONNA GO.
MAYBE IT'S RUDE NOT TO GO AFTER ACCEPT-ING THE TICKET...
...BUT WITH EVERYTHING RYUNOSUKE'S GOING THROUGH...

SORRY, KURAMA.
HEY!
THERE SHE IS!
TARGET LOCKED. ♡
Verb Construction - Infinitive
Construction - Adverbial Phrase
from home ?
sence ?
YOU UNDER-STAND SO FAR?
YES.

I WAS SURPRISED WHEN I HEARD YOU HAD REMEDIAL CLASSES.
YOU WERE ALWAYS A GOOD STUDENT WHEN YOU TRIED.
IT'S MOSTLY BECAUSE OF YOUR ATTENDANCE RECORD, RIGHT?
Your grades aren't too bad.
MAYBE YOU'RE SPENDING TOO MUCH TIME WITH MISS SAKURA...
MA'AM.
CAN WE JUST KEEP GOING?

TUP
SHEESH.
YOU GET ALL CRANKY AT THE VERY MENTION OF MISS SAKURA.
AND TO THINK I WAS GOING TO LET YOU IN ON A SECRET.
I DON'T WANNA HEAR IT.
KILK KILK
MISS SAKURA...
...IS SEEING ANOTHER BOY TODAY.

HUH?
IT ISN'T JUST TODAY.
I'VE SEEN HER BEFORE...
...WITH OTHER BOYS.
I WASN'T SURE IF I SHOULD TELL YOU OR NOT...
...BUT IF SHE'S CHEATING ON YOU, RYU...
...
OH YEAH?
TAF

PROJECT MUCH, DONCHA?
I DON'T NEED THIS CRAP. CAN YOU GET BACK TO TEACHING?
OR ARE WE DONE HERE?
IF SCHOOL'S OVER, I'M LEAVING.
CHAK
SHF
I THOUGHT YOU'D SAY THAT.
BUT...

Dear Ryoko,
...CAN YOU STILL LAUGH IT OFF AFTER SEEING THIS?
KYAAAA

HEY! HEY! STOP!
WHAT'RE YOU DOING?
FWAP
HERE, GET ON.
Should we call the cops?
They're just fooling around.
SHOVE
HUH?
WHOA!
ABDUCTION COMPLETE. ♡
HUH?
Ready to ride?
Roger.
WHO ARE THESE PEOPLE?

IF YOU TRY TO MOVE YOU'LL FALL AND KILL YOUR-SELF.
Just hang on tight.
HUH?
Kill myself?
WAIT A SEC!
WHAT IS THIS? WHERE ARE YOU TAKING ME?
VROOOM
C'MON, YOU KNOW WHERE.
A VERY HAPPY PLACE. ♡
LIKE HEAVEN?
STOP!!
VOOOSH
SHAAA

STUDIO ROT
B♭
C
HM
HM
Am
B♭
WARMING UP. →→→
WE'RE READY FOR SOUND CHECK WHENEVER YOU GUYS ARE.
HEY! YOU'D BETTER NOT MESS UP!!
WHAK
OW!
YOU DON'T WANNA MAKE A FOOL OF YOURSELF IN FRONT OF RYON-RYON!
Sitting on the floor.
THANKS.
YEAH...
...BUT WE DON'T EVEN KNOW IF SHE'S COMING!
YOU KNOW YOU WANT HER TO. ♡
YOU KNOW YOU'RE HOPING SHE DOES. ♡

DON'T WORRY. SHE'LL BE HERE.
SHE SAID YESTERDAY WAS A COINCIDENCE, BUT SHE TOTALLY CAME TO SEE YOU.
SHE'S DEFINITELY INTO YOU.
RIGHT, SHU?
Ha ha... YEAH.
SHE'LL COME.
SEE? IF SHU SAYS SO, IT'S TRUE!
WE'LL SEE YOU GUYS ONSTAGE!
...
HOW CAN YOU BE SO SURE?
Huh? DUDE, TRUST ME.
I'M NOT SO SURE SHE'S INTO YOU, THOUGH...
YOU DON'T HAVE TO TELL ME THAT.

HE TOLD ME NOT TO WORRY, BUT I COULDN'T STOP.
...BUT I COULDN'T STOP.
I COULDN'T JUST SIT THERE AND DO NOTHING...
I COULDN'T JUST SIT THERE AND DO NOTHING...
BUT YOU CHEERED ME UP.
BUT YOU CHEERED ME UP.
SHE SEEMED SO SAD...
...BUT SHE'S ALL WRAPPED UP IN HER BOY-FRIEND.
I'M NOT EVEN IN HER SIGHTS.
SO YOU'RE JUST GONNA SULK AND GIVE UP?
WHAT?
CONCERT

STEAL HER FROM THAT JERK.
THAT'S WHAT WE CALL ***BEING A WUSS.***
IF THE GIRL YOU LIKE IS SAD, WHY NOT MAKE HER HAPPY?
OR...
...DON'T YOU THINK YOU CAN BRING IT?
TAK
I'M GOING OUT FOR SOME AIR.

STEAL HER FROM THAT JERK.
BRRRRRR
Enjoy the ride?
WE'RE HERE! ♡
...
HI-YAH!!
THWAK
Enjoy this!!
ACK!!
KIDNAP-PER!!
WHERE AM I?

WHO THE HELL *ARE* YOU GUYS, ANYWAY?
CALM DOWN, RYON-RYON!
WHEW
ALL WILL BE REVEALED WHEN YOU SEE MY FACE!
Ryon-Ryon?
SEE?
...
WHO ARE YOU?
C'MON!
I WAS WITH KURA YESTER-DAY!!
You don't remember me?
HUH? Were you?
I ASKED THEM TO BRING YOU HERE.
WHAT?
Have a good ride?
Hey! SHU!

THANKS, GUYS.
HIM!
I remember him!
NO PROB.
IT WAS ON OUR WAY.
My hair's a mess.
HAVE A GOOD SHOW, MAN.
THANKS.
SHOW?
SO THAT MEANS...
WAAH
STUDIO ROT
WAAH
THE SHOW STARTS SOON.
...WE'RE AT THE CLUB!

WE'RE PLAYING SECOND. SO GRAB A DRINK.
Chill.
ARE YOU FOR REAL?
I DON'T BELIEVE THIS!
YOU GRABBED ME AND DRAGGED ME HERE?
WHAT IF I'D HAD SOME-WHERE IMPORTANT TO BE?
I'M GOING HOME!
SORRY.
I JUST REALLY WANTED YOU TO BE HERE.

KURA'S NEVER WORKED THIS HARD BEFORE.
WE'RE FEELING GOOD ABOUT THIS.
I WANTED YOU TO SEE HIM.
CAN YOU STICK AROUND FOR JUST ONE SONG?
YOUR BOYFRIEND WON'T LOSE IT OVER ONE SONG, RIGHT?
SHU!
Time for sound check!
I GOTTA GO.
...
Hey... Who's that?
Forget it.
Let's go.

(4) Last note!

Kurama's friends call Ryoko "Ryon-Ryon." I took the nickname from a letter I got!! Thanks, M-Hara from Hokkaido!!

Sorry! Heh!

I'm sorry I used it without permission... I just liked it so much. I'd like to take this opportunity to ask for belated permission.

**I took the liberty of using your idea!!**
(Please approve retroactively!)
I'm really sorry.

If you don't mind your words being stolen out of nowhere, I'll be waiting for your letters.

B.O.D.Y.
c/o VIZ Media, LLC
P.O. Box 77010
San Francisco, CA 94107

Ao Mimori

Keep 'em coming!! I'll be waiting!

Kyaa Kyaa

Dear Ryoko,
Come by if you have time. You might have some fun. I'll be waiting.
Kurama

WHAT IS THIS?
I FOUND IT.
HUH? Show?
SQUIK
THERE WAS A TICKET FOR A SHOW WITH THAT NOTE.
SHE'S PROBABLY...
...AT THAT BOY'S SHOW ABOUT NOW.
IT WAS DATED FOR TODAY.
SHE NEVER TOLD YOU?
WHAT'RE YOU GONNA DO TODAY?
I'LL JUST GO HOME AND DO SOME HOMEWORK.
TAF
WHATEVER.

SHE WOULDN'T GO OFF SOMEWHERE WITHOUT TELLING ME.
THEN...
...DO YOU KNOW WHO THIS "KURAMA" IS?
AND DID YOU KNOW SHE'S FRIENDS WITH A BOY WITH BLEACHED HAIR?
I SAW THEM TOGETHER JUST THE OTHER DAY...
...THE DAY WE WERE CALLED INTO THE PRINCIPAL'S OFFICE!

'BYE!
BE CAREFUL!
ASK HER YOURSELF IF YOU THINK I'M LYING.
Come by if you have time.
You might have some fun.
I'll be waiting.
Kurama
I SUGGEST YOU GO SEE FOR YOURSELF.

STUDIO ROT
JACK DA
DRIN
IT'S SO LOUD...
JUST ONE SONG.
...
I GUESS IT WOULDN'T HURT.
I'LL WATCH QUIETLY AND DUCK OUT AFTER-WARDS.
DRESSI
KURA!
DAKKA

RYON-RYON'S HERE!!
PBBT
?!
Koff
SERIOUSLY?
I SWEAR. ♡
I JUST LOOKED OUT FROM THE STAGE AND SHE WAS STANDING ALONE IN THE BACK!!
Alone
I can't believe it! She really came!
YOU GUYS ARE UP IN FIVE MINUTES.
WE'LL BE RIGHT THERE!!
Thanks!
Let's do this!!
Yeah!! Let's go!!
...
BDMP BDMP BDMP
SHOW HER WHAT YOU'VE GOT.

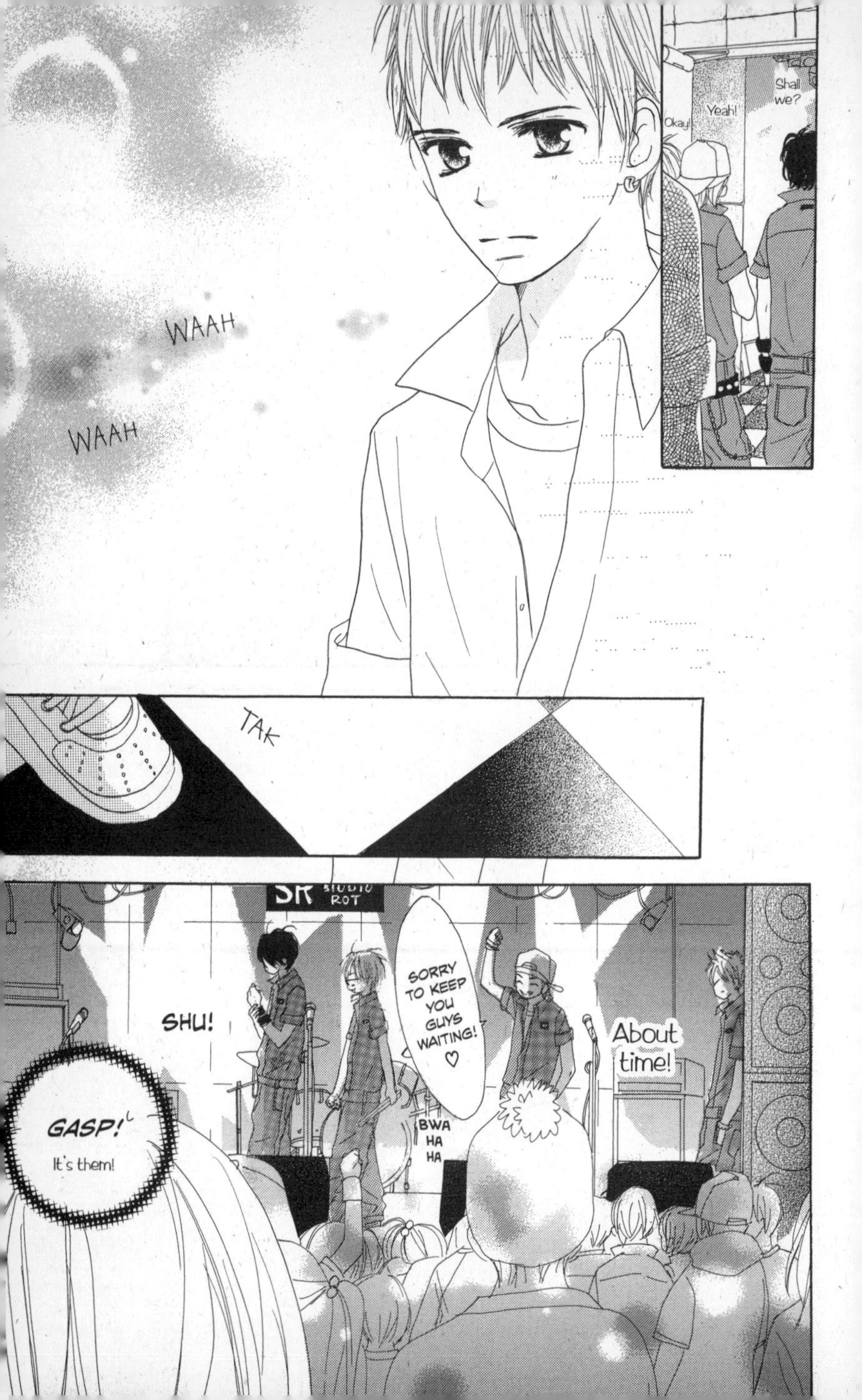
Shall we?
Yeah!
Okay!
WAAH
WAAH
TAK
SR STUDIO ROT
About time!
SORRY TO KEEP YOU GUYS WAITING! ♡
SHU!
BWA HA HA
GASP!
It's them!

KURA !!
Hope you practiced!
SHUT UP!
I'll kick your ass!
What-ever!
JUST DON'T SCREW UP TONIGHT!
HA HA HA HA
HOPE HE WASN'T JUST BEING MODEST...
YEEK
NOW I'M KIND OF CURIOUS.
TK
TK
WHAT?
If you hear my horrible guitar playing...

Thanks to Koenji at Club Liner
(www.club-liner.net) for research assistance.

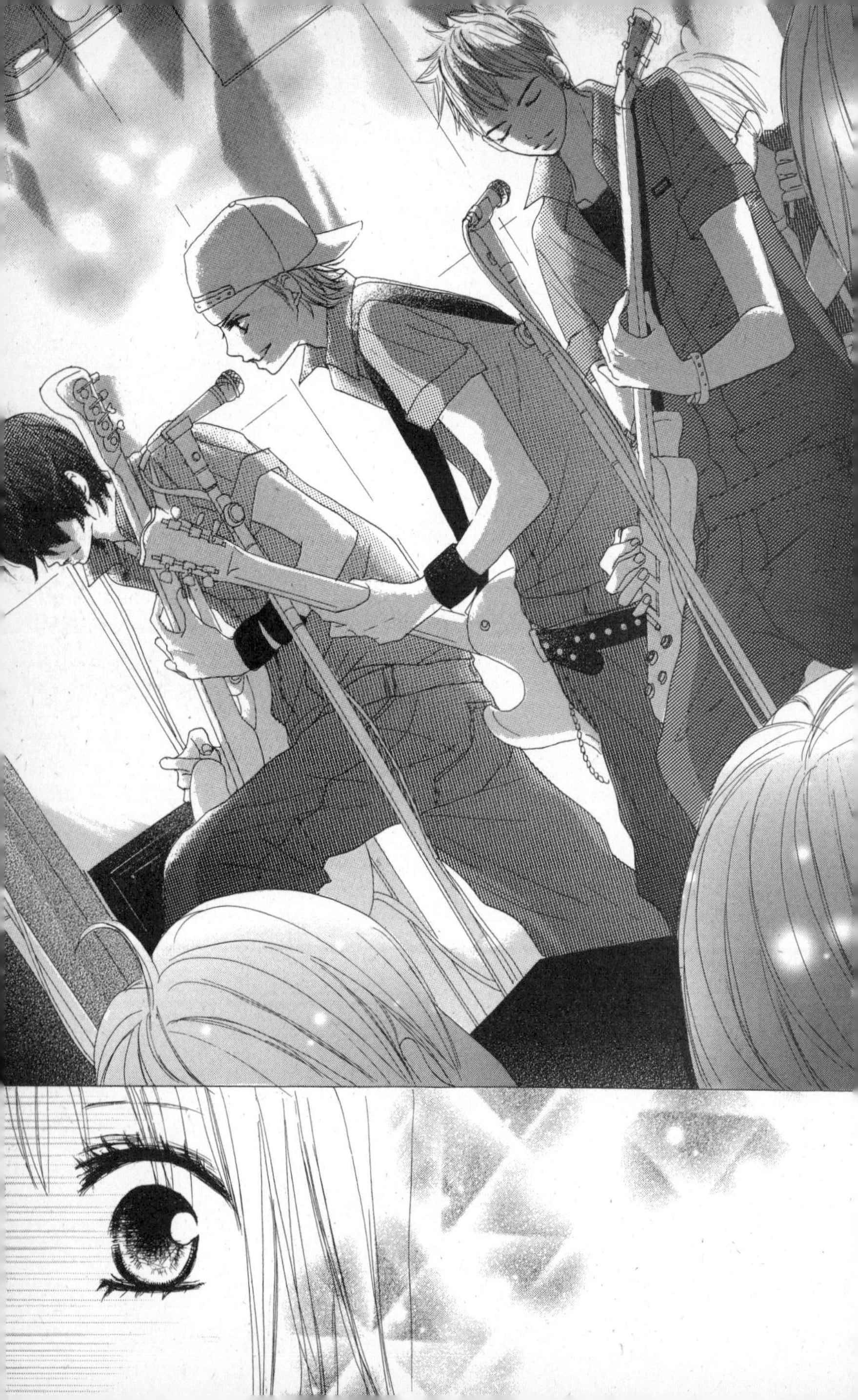

WHOA.
NO WAY!
THEY'RE NOT BAD AT ALL.
IN FACT, THEY'RE PRETTY GOOD!

WAH WAH
WHEW ...
WELL, WE'VE REACHED THE MIDDLE OF OUR SET...
...AND, AS I'M SURE SOME OF YOU HAVE ALREADY NOTICED...
...BE-LIEVE IT OR NOT...
...KURA HASN'T SCREWED UP YET!
HUH ?
WHOA!
WOW...

WHAT'S WRONG, KURA?
You okay?
That's not like you!
Just relax, buddy!
...
HOW BAD IS HE USU-ALLY?
I'M NOT SURPRISED.
IT'S 'CAUSE TONIGHT...
...KURA'S CRUSH...
...RYON-RYON IS HERE. ♡
HEY!!!
What's he saying about me?
Who's Ryon-Ryon?
Where is she?
OKAY, QUIET!!
WAAH
WAAH

I'D BETTER GET OUTTA HERE...
DON'T YOU HAVE ANYTHING TO SAY, KURA?
To your honey? ♥
TAK
HUH?
HELL NO! LEAVE HER AL...
THAT'S WHAT WE CALL BEING A WUSS.
DON'T YOU THINK YOU CAN BRING IT?
Excuse me...
GRP
WHY NOT MAKE HER HAPPY?

ACTUALLY, I DO WANNA SAY SOMETHING.
Say it!!
Go Kura!!
ha ha ha
WHAT?
I TOLD YOU I'D BE WAITING.
BUT I WANNA SAY MORE THAN THAT.
STUDIO R

I WON'T EVER MAKE YOU CRY.
NO REENTRY
I WON'T EVER MAKE YOU SAD.
I WON'T EVER MAKE YOU FEEL INSE-CURE.
I'LL PROTECT YOU FROM ANYBODY WHO TRIES TO HURT YOU.

MISS RYOKO SAKURA...
CHAK
...PLEASE BE MY GIRLFRIEND.

WAAAAAH
Way to go, Kura!!
WAAAAH
SEE?

Whoa! Holy crap!
I WASN'T LYING, WAS I?
What're you gonna tell him, Ryoko?
Say some-thing!!
KURAMA!
KURAMA!
YEAH!


...To Be Continued.

# RADIO RECORDING DIARY PART 2!!

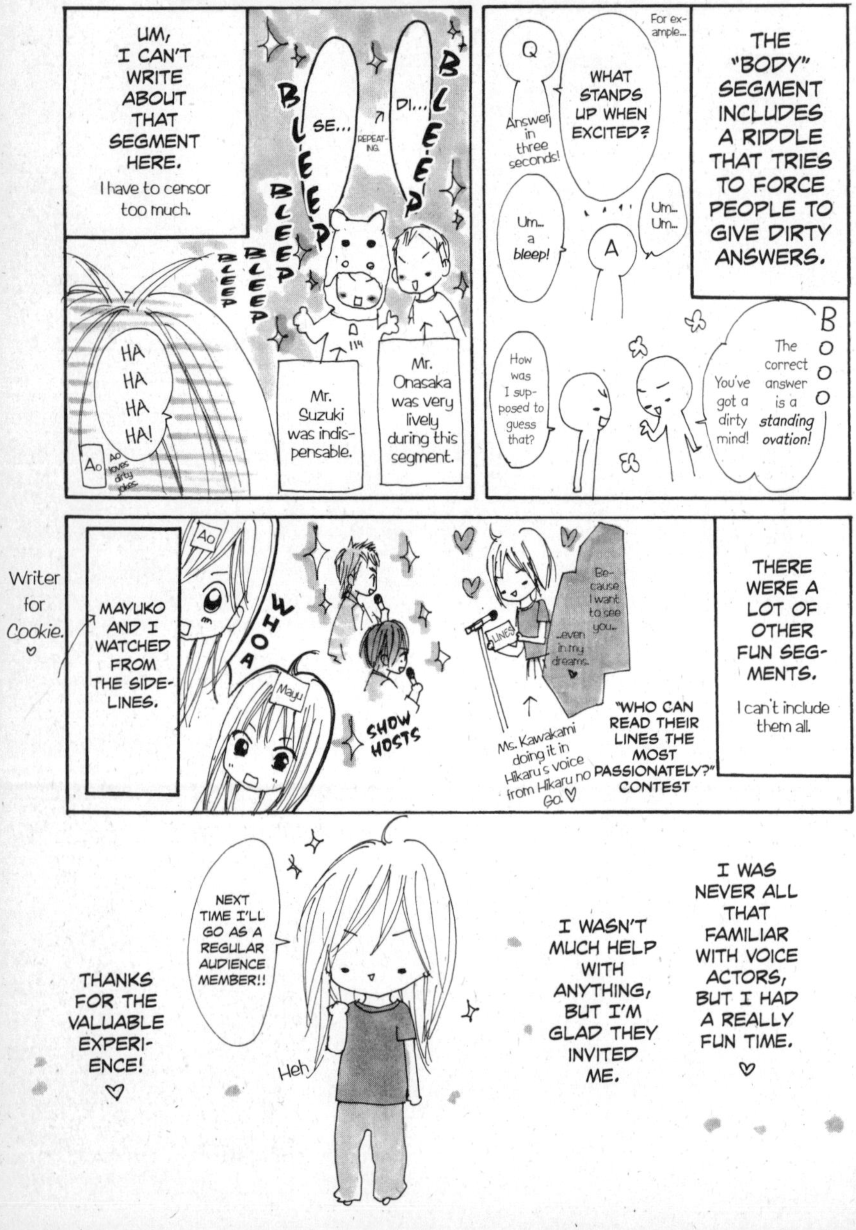
UM, I CAN'T WRITE ABOUT THAT SEGMENT HERE.
I have to censor too much.
SE...
REPEATING.
DI...
BLEEP
BLEEP
BLEEP
BLEEP
BLEEP
HA HA HA HA!
Ao
Ao loves dirty jokes
Mr. Suzuki was indispensable.
Mr. Onasaka was very lively during this segment.
THE "BODY" SEGMENT INCLUDES A RIDDLE THAT TRIES TO FORCE PEOPLE TO GIVE DIRTY ANSWERS.
For example...
Q
WHAT STANDS UP WHEN EXCITED?
Answer in three seconds!
Um... a bleep!
A
Um... Um...
How was I supposed to guess that?
You've got a dirty mind!
The correct answer is a standing ovation!
BOOOO
Writer for Cookie.
MAYUKO AND I WATCHED FROM THE SIDELINES.
Ao
Mayu
WHOA
SHOW HOSTS
LINES
Because I want to see you...
...even in my dreams.
Ms. Kawakami doing it in Hikaru's voice from Hikaru no Go.
"WHO CAN READ THEIR LINES THE MOST PASSIONATELY?" CONTEST
THERE WERE A LOT OF OTHER FUN SEGMENTS.
I can't include them all.
NEXT TIME I'LL GO AS A REGULAR AUDIENCE MEMBER!!
Heh
I WAS NEVER ALL THAT FAMILIAR WITH VOICE ACTORS, BUT I HAD A REALLY FUN TIME.
I WASN'T MUCH HELP WITH ANYTHING, BUT I'M GLAD THEY INVITED ME.
THANKS FOR THE VALUABLE EXPERIENCE!

# DRAMA CD RECORDING DIARY

INABA
SÔICHIRO HOSHI
RAN
MINAMI TAKAYAMA
RYOKO
TOMOKO KAWAKAMI
FUJI
JUNICHI SUWABE
GUY
INAGAKI
TEACHER
HORIKAWA
SHINOBU
TATSUHISA SUZUKI
YUKI
RURI ASANO
ASUKA
MIKI NAGASAWA

THERE WERE SO MANY TOP-NOTCH VOICE ACTORS.
ALL THE CHARACTERS TURNED OUT GREAT.
LISTEN AND JUDGE FOR YOURSELF!
AREN'T WE GOING OVER-BOARD?
HARMONIOUS ATMOSPHERE
I HEAR CONAN'S VOICE...
What's going on over there?




※ Minami Takayama plays Conan in the Case Closed anime.

AMIDST ALL THAT...
WE DON'T HAVE ENOUGH PEOPLE FOR THE CROWD SCENES, SO JOIN IN IF YOU LIKE.
Are you sure?
ER... OKAY.
I HAD TO JOIN ALL THOSE GREAT ACTRESSES AS A MEMBER OF THE CROWD.
I should've just said no...
※ We had to improvise a crowd talking casually.
H... HI... ...GUYS.
ACT LIKE YOU'RE WIPED OUT AFTER A RACE.
← DIRECTOR
WE'RE READY! ROLL!
Everybody else did it with ease.
I'm tired...
My feet hurt...
...
What am I doing here?
Are the boys done yet?
AO... ...CANNOT IMPROVISE.
I told you not to do it!
AND WHEN I FINALLY OPENED MY MOUTH, THIS IS WHAT CAME OUT...
I'M HUNGRY!
Too loud.
OH NO! WHAT WAS THAT?
IN MY MIND...
YEAH.
LET'S GRAB A BITE ON THE WAY HOME.
POP
!!
THEN MS. ASANO JOINED IN ON OUR CONVERSATION.
WHAT DO YOU GUYS WANNA EAT?
What should we get?
Ms. Takayama saved me...
She's so amazing...
THEY WERE SO KIND TO ME...
THANK YOU VERY MUCH.

And that is how, with the help of many people, we were able to complete the CD. To the cast and crew, thank you very much.

All I want now is for plenty of people to hear it. If you're curious, pick up a copy. You can buy it online.

It includes a bonus manga featuring Ryunosuke and Ryoko, so check it out.

B.O.D.Y.

## So what do you think?

All of the side projects are done and the story's turning pretty turbulent, but I'll keep doing my best.

I couldn't share any mail in this volume, but I'm hoping to include some in the next volume, so keep the letters coming.

That's about it for now. See you soon!

I'll see you in volume 9!

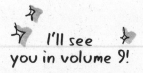

2006.9.20 Ao Mimori

Next Volume! NEXT COMIC COMING SOON!

IT'S NOT GONNA END THIS WAY.
I DIDN'T CHEAT ON RYUNOSUKE.
HE'S A HOST.
YOU CAN DO WHATEVER YOU WANT WITH ME.
MAYBE YOU'D BE HAPPIER WITH THAT GUY.
B.O.D.Y.

VOLUME 9 COMING SOON!

# B.O.D.Y. Language

**Page 56, panel 4-5:** katsu sandwich, melon bread, yakisoba sandwich
*Katsu sando* is a sandwich containing *tonkatsu*, breaded and fried pork cutlet. It's a common item in bento boxes. Melon bread is a cookie-topped pastry designed to look like a melon; it's not necessarily melon flavored. A yakisoba sandwich is made with *yakisoba*, or fried noodles. It's a little like eating spaghetti on a bun.

**Page 130, Author's Note:** Kudan Kaikan
A hotel, restaurant and convention-hall complex in Tokyo.

**Page 132, panel 1:** *Shûei Gakuen Otome Kenkyûbu*
As mentioned in volume 7, Ao Mimori appeared as a guest on this Internet radio show, which often features guests from the manga and anime industries. The show includes a regular segment called "Body," making her appearance especially appropriate.

**Page 175, panel 3:** *Hikaru no Go*
Popular manga and anime created by Yumi Hotta and Takeshi Obata. Hikaru, a teenage boy, becomes involved in the game of go after awakening the ghost of Fujiwara-no-Sai, a master go player from the Heian era. Tomoko Kawakami is the voice of Hikaru in the *Hikaru no Go* anime.

**Author's Commentary**

This is the 14th volume of manga I've drawn... As you can see above, the little character I've been drawing since my debut has been made into a key chain! When my first comic was published, I never could've imagined the day when my doodle would become adorable merchandise. It's all thanks to you readers! Thank you so much! ♡♡♡

Ao Mimori began creating manga during her junior year of college, and her work debuted when she was only 23. *B.O.D.Y.*, her third series, was first published in *Bessatsu Margaret* in 2003 and is also available in Japanese as an audio CD. Her other work includes *Sonnano Koi Jyanai* (That's Not Love), *Anta Nanka Iranai* (I Don't Need You), *Dakishimetaiyo Motto* (I Want to Hold You More), *I LOVE YOU* and *Kamisama no Iu Toori* (As the God of Death Dictates).

**B.O.D.Y. VOL 8**
Shojo Beat Edition

STORY & ART BY
**AO MIMORI**

Translation/Joe Yamazaki
Touch-up Art & Lettering/HudsonYards
Design/Sean Lee
Editor/Shaenon K. Garrity

VP, Production/Alvin Lu
VP, Sales & Product Marketing/Gonzalo Ferreyra
VP, Creative/Linda Espinosa
Publisher/Hyoe Narita



Printed in Canada

Published by VIZ Media, LLC
P.O. Box 77010
San Francisco, CA 94107

10 9 8 7 6 5 4 3 2 1
First printing, February 2010

www.viz.com www.shojobeat.com

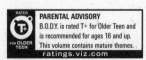

RATED T+ FOR OLDER TEEN

**PARENTAL ADVISORY**
B.O.D.Y. is rated T+ for Older Teen and is recommended for ages 16 and up. This volume contains mature themes.
ratings.viz.com

# Tell us what you think about Shojo Beat Manga!



Our survey is now available online. Go to:

***shojobeat.com/mangasurvey***

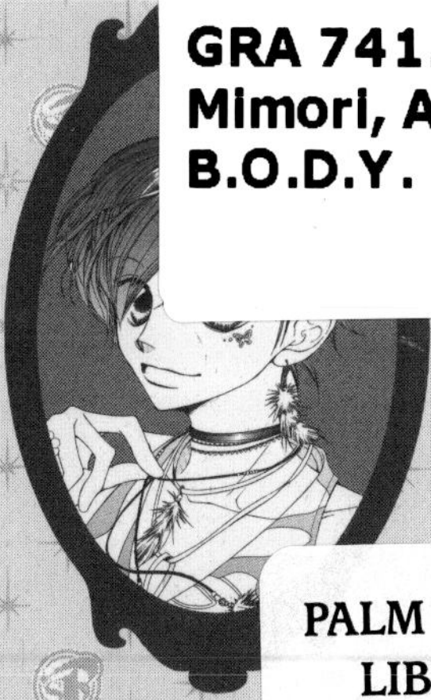

## Help us make our product offerings better!



THE REAL DRAMA BEGINS IN...